HAL•LEONARD
INSTRUMENTAL
PLAY-ALONG

AUDIO
ACCESS
INCLUDED

PLAYBACK+
Speed • Pitch • Balance • Loop

CELLO

CHRISTMAS
CLASSICS

Angels We Have Heard on High	2
Bring a Torch, Jeannette, Isabella	3
Coventry Carol	4
Fum, Fum, Fum	5
Go, Tell It on the Mountain	6
God Rest Ye Merry, Gentlemen	7
Here We Come A-Caroling	8
The Holly and the Ivy	9
I Saw Three Ships	10
Jingle Bells	11
O Come, All Ye Faithful	12
O Holy Night	13
Silent Night	14
Still, Still, Still	15
What Child Is This?	16

Audio arrangements by Peter Deneff

To access audio visit:
www.halleonard.com/mylibrary

Enter Code
1650-4985-0941-4285

ISBN 978-1-4950-7063-1

HAL•LEONARD®
CORPORATION

7777 W. BLUEMOUND RD. P.O. BOX 13819 MILWAUKEE, WI 53213

In Australia Contact:
Hal Leonard Australia Pty. Ltd.
4 Lentara Court
Cheltenham, Victoria, 3192 Australia
Email: ausadmin@halleonard.com.au

Copyright © 2016 by HAL LEONARD CORPORATION
International Copyright Secured   All Rights Reserved

For all works contained herein:
Unauthorized copying, arranging, adapting, recording, Internet posting, public performance,
or other distribution of the printed or recorded music in this publication is an infringement of copyright.
Infringers are liable under the law.

Visit Hal Leonard Online at
www.halleonard.com

ANGELS WE HAVE HEARD ON HIGH

CELLO

Traditional French Carol

Copyright © 2016 by HAL LEONARD CORPORATION
International Copyright Secured   All Rights Reserved

BRING A TORCH, JEANNETTE, ISABELLA

CELLO

17th Century French Provençal Carol

Copyright © 2016 by HAL LEONARD CORPORATION
International Copyright Secured   All Rights Reserved

COVENTRY CAROL

CELLO

Traditional English Melody

Copyright © 2016 by HAL LEONARD CORPORATION
International Copyright Secured   All Rights Reserved

FUM, FUM, FUM

CELLO

Traditional Catalonian Carol

Copyright © 2016 by HAL LEONARD CORPORATION
International Copyright Secured   All Rights Reserved

GO, TELL IT ON THE MOUNTAIN

CELLO

African-American Spiritual

Copyright © 2016 by HAL LEONARD CORPORATION
International Copyright Secured   All Rights Reserved

GOD REST YE MERRY, GENTLEMEN

CELLO

Traditional English Carol

Copyright © 2016 by HAL LEONARD CORPORATION
International Copyright Secured   All Rights Reserved

HERE WE COME A-CAROLING

CELLO

Traditional

Copyright © 2016 by HAL LEONARD CORPORATION
International Copyright Secured   All Rights Reserved

THE HOLLY AND THE IVY

CELLO

18th Century English Carol

Copyright © 2016 by HAL LEONARD CORPORATION
International Copyright Secured   All Rights Reserved

I SAW THREE SHIPS

CELLO

Traditional English Carol

Copyright © 2016 by HAL LEONARD CORPORATION
International Copyright Secured   All Rights Reserved

JINGLE BELLS

Words and Music by
J. PIERPONT

CELLO

Copyright © 2016 by HAL LEONARD CORPORATION
International Copyright Secured   All Rights Reserved

O COME, ALL YE FAITHFUL

CELLO

Music by JOHN FRANCIS WADE

Copyright © 2016 by HAL LEONARD CORPORATION
International Copyright Secured   All Rights Reserved

O HOLY NIGHT

CELLO

French Words by PLACIDE CAPPEAU
English Words by JOHN S. DWIGHT
Music by ADOLPHE ADAM

Copyright © 2016 by HAL LEONARD CORPORATION
International Copyright Secured   All Rights Reserved

SILENT NIGHT

CELLO

Words by JOSEPH MOHR
Music by FRANZ X. GRUBER

Copyright © 2016 by HAL LEONARD CORPORATION
International Copyright Secured   All Rights Reserved

STILL, STILL, STILL

CELLO

Salzburg Melody, c.1819

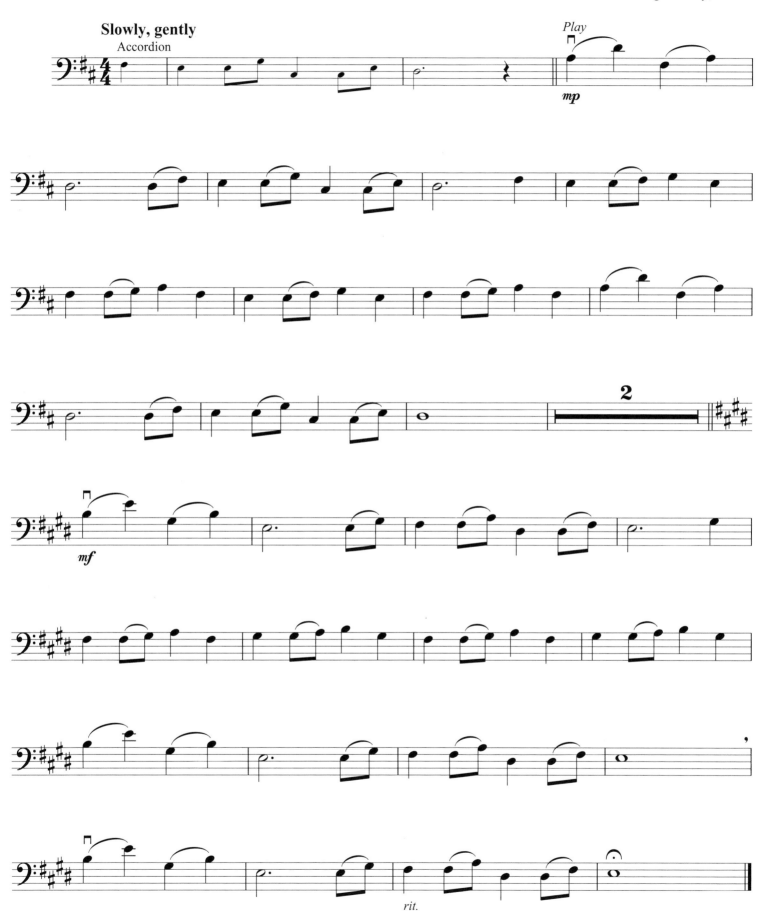

Copyright © 2016 by HAL LEONARD CORPORATION
International Copyright Secured   All Rights Reserved

WHAT CHILD IS THIS?

CELLO

16th Century English Melody

Copyright © 2016 by HAL LEONARD CORPORATION
International Copyright Secured   All Rights Reserved